Mindset Mastery: Unleashing Your Inner Victor in Corporate Adversities

Embrace Your True Identity, Reclaim Your Power, Ignite a Global Revolution

Saskia Christian

Copyright © Saskia Christian, 2024

All Rights Reserved

ISBN 979-8-89443-949-5

Book Cover designed by:

Farabee Publishing. Chandler, Arizona 85224

Without limiting the rights under copyright reserved above, no part of this publication may be reproduced, stored in, or introduced into a retrieval system, or transmitted, in any form or by any means (electronic, mechanical, photocopying, recording, or otherwise), without the prior written permission of both the copyright owner and the above publisher of this book.

The scanning, uploading, and distribution of this book via the internet or via any other means without the permission of the publisher is illegal and punishable by law. Please purchase only authorized editions and do not participate in or encourage piracy of copyrighted materials. your support of the author's rights is appreciated.

Forward

Unveil the transformative strategies within the pages of "Mindset Mastery: Unleashing Your Inner Victor in Corporate Adversities."

Join author Saskia on a remarkable journey of personal empowerment and liberation as she delves into her own redemption story of resilience and reclaiming power from the marginalization of talent.

This book is a powerful call to action for professionals across industries who have experienced the stifling grip of mediocrity in the workplace.

Saskia boldly addresses the destruction, undervaluation, and societal loss that occur when talent-rich individuals remain trapped in a cycle of unfulfilled potential.

It is time to break free from the chains of victimhood and embrace the path to undercover victory.

Table of Contents

Turning The Tables 8
   From Corporate Victim To Undercover Victor .. 8
   From Victim To Triumph 10
   Full Of Potential, Stuck In A Box......................... 14
   Cultural and Educational Bias............................. 16
   Skewed Meritocracy System 17
   Relational Currency 18

Life As A Talent Exclusion Victim............................... 19

Are You Paddling Against The Current?................... 21

What Is An Undercover Victor? 23

The Victim To Undercover Victor Transformation . 25
      Resilience 26
      Confidence.. 27
      Strategy 29

Next Steps.. 32
      Putting It Into Practice 32
      Activate Your UV Superpowers........................... 32
      Practicing Resilience.. 33
      Boost Your Self-Confidence 33
      Strategic Integration.. 34

Saskia Christian 35

Notes 38

Dedication

To the Unsung Heroes

This book is dedicated to the talented professionals who have yet to realize the greatness within themselves. It is for those who have been held back by the limitations imposed by their environment, but deep down, possess the potential for extraordinary achievements.

In the corporate world, so many of you have been labeled as underdogs, constantly overlooked, and underestimated. But let me tell you something: within each of you lies a hidden reservoir of strength, resilience, and untapped potential.

This book is here to help you unleash that power and transform your mindset to become the undercover victor you were always meant to be.

I see your struggles, your battles against self-doubt and the limitations imposed upon you. But know this: you are not alone.

This book is a guiding light, a roadmap to help you navigate the challenges and rise above the odds stacked against you. It provides a formula for mindset transformation, offering practical strategies, insights, and inspiration to help you break free from the underdog mentality and embrace triumphant living in your professional life.

Through these pages, you will discover how to cultivate an unwavering belief in your abilities, how to leverage your unique strengths, and how to seize opportunities that others might overlook.

You will learn how to overcome the barriers that have held you back and step into your true potential. It is time to rewrite your narrative and rewrite the rules of success.

To all the unsung heroes, it's time to shine. Embrace the journey ahead, for within you lies the power to create your own success story. Believe in yourself, trust in your abilities, and know that the world is waiting for your greatness to be unleashed.

Here's to your transformation, to your triumph, and to the victorious life that awaits you.

With utmost admiration and unwavering belief,

Saskia Christian, MS, PMP, CTC, TRLC

Founder @BoostThru International Best-Selling Author, Motivational Speaker, Trauma Healing & Resilience Life Coach, Executive Contributor to Brainz Magazine.

Turning The Tables

From Corporate Victim To Undercover Victor

As a child living in Guyana, my parents and relatives instilled into me the importance of a sound education and great work ethic. They would said, "Education will take you places, Saskia. The sky's the limit!"

My lineage includes University scholars, draftsmen, and engineers. So, it only seemed natural that I would choose the academic path of excellence. Though I lacked the luxury of daily school lunch stipend, faced frequent water shortages, and was entertained by relatives' folktales during electricity outages better known as "blackouts," my family didn't focus on our limitations.

I knew deep down that my purpose was much bigger than my temporary condition. After all, I was simply not raised to feel less valuable or incapable than others who had more.

I saw shining examples of strong determination in my own family. My immediate relatives surely did not have the means to live comfortably yet believed that a better life was on the way. They knew that education was the only way to get there and invested their last dollars to purchase the required textbooks for the family's youth.

That bright future awaiting would sparkle before our very eyes when our successful distant relatives visited from abroad with all their credentials.

Those cousins had managed to escape the limitations of a poor third- world country by attending university on academic scholarships in the

U.S. and England. They raved about their corporate achievements and elevated standard of living. Yes, education fueled by a strong work ethic surely paved the way for them to experience all of life's goodness. It was a tradition in our immediate family for the children to reveal their school report cards to those accomplished cousins.

We anxiously awaited their words of encouragement and most importantly, gifts based on our grade performance. They fed us audacious hope for a better tomorrow. We dared to dream and dreamed big!

After hearing those testimonies about all the life-changing possibilities success brings, I couldn't resist daydreaming about how I could be exceptional by using that good ole' reliable platform of elevation called education to change the life trajectory for myself and my immediate family. I couldn't resist being intrigued by science and the practicality engineering brought to the world.

I loved chemistry and adored math. I had a longing to pursue an engineering discipline that would carry on my love for those subjects and enable me to add the most value and relevance to society. The coveted field of chemical engineering and its wide industrial application convinced me to pursue that path. I had that unrelenting fire burning within to stand out even though I knew there would be many obstacles along the way.

From Victim To Triumph

My latter high school years were the beginning of a redemption story that ultimately prepared me to conquer life's adversities years later. It all started the day I collected those dreaded Caribbean Examinations Council (CXC) examination results. That CXC exam is the equivalent of the Scholastic Assessment Test (SAT) in the U.S., and it would become the most defining moment of my life.

Everyone knew the importance of a child "making the grade" on the CXC exam. A teenager's future and overall quality of life were described based on their performance in that one examination.

The high emphasis on that examination and its determination of my life outcome placed tremendous pressure on me. I was horrified about the prospect of being labeled a failure if I didn't pass.

Consumed with fear, I chose to take the journey to the school grounds to collect my results with a classmate to encourage my spirit along the way. Unlike me, she was excited because she knew she would succeed. I was silent.

As I endured an agonizing wait in the results line, I was overtaken by huge sighs of relief and celebratory outbursts from my fellow classmates as they opened their results in the corridor. I was finally handed the white envelope with my grade slip enclosed. I was terrified to open "my future" so I slipped it into my pocket and hustled to find a safe spot far away from my classmates and teachers. I finally mustered up enough strength to open the envelope. My hands trembled, crumpling the paper so badly that I could barely read the grades.

I failed.

I was in complete disbelief. How could I move forward from not meeting the expectations of my family? How would I overcome such a low moment in my life? I had let down myself and my loved ones. I slipped the grades back into my pocket and hurried down the stairs.

I was too ashamed to face the barrage of questions from my friends regarding my deplorable results. I contemplated my life on that long, miserable journey home. I went into my room, threw myself on the bed, and burst into tears.

My Mom reviewed the results, took a long pause, and then started to console me about my future.

She promised to do all she could to give me an opportunity to succeed.

After several weeks, my mom took the lead in the battle for my future and went to see my high school principal. She believed that she could lobby for me to repeat the course and retake the exam. The principal said she had several exam retakers and didn't have room for me. My mom couldn't understand why someone with a good attitude like me would be denied a second chance.

Later she inquired at another highly rated high school and was successful in getting me accepted for a retake exam. I was welcomed into that setting and was surrounded by teachers and classmates who boosted my self- confidence. They motivated me to discover my inner strengths and rise above adversity. We studied and practiced questions together. We encouraged and empowered each other.

I no longer shudder at taking examinations. My confidence led me to conquer anything ahead.

A year later, I bounced back from that heartbreaking defeat. Because I was given a fighting chance, I channeled all that embarrassment into aspiration and joy. I passed all my CXC subjects with course distinctions. That experience taught me the power of resilience.

As I reflect, I can't help but to ponder on all that could have been stolen from me.

If my upbringing hadn't taught me the power of perseverance, if I didn't have a mother who was willing and able to advocate for me, leading to a new, healthier learning environment, I would not have had an opportunity to be victorious over those CXC examinations. My outcome could have been like those in my community left behind to struggle financially with unfulfilled dreams.

As I look back there were three major factors that led to the transformation of my dreams into reality:

- Support provided in my home and new high school environment.

- Steadfast commitment to education as a platform of elevation.

- An ingrained power of resilience.

- A can-do attitude from being raised with a deep sense of belief.

Six years later, I was able to achieve that momentous milestone of becoming a chemical engineer. Today, I'm nearly two decades into a successful career that includes passing the notoriously difficult Project Management Professional (PMP) certification exam. While statistics are not disclosed, some project expert surveys estimate the failure rate as high as 50 percent.

Learning those test-taking strategies sure did pay off! I'm also a mentor and a visionary with an excellent track record of influencing across all levels of high-tech organizational functions. But it wasn't always that way.

There were times when I felt like I struggled to find my place and prove my value. Little did I know my greatest personal challenge would become one of the greatest sources of competitive edge for me professionally.

Full Of Potential, Stuck In A Box

When I look back at the redemption journey of my CXC exam, I see how monumental both strategy and environmental factors were in securing my success on that exam retake. I realize that I was smart enough to pass the first time around but had not yet cultivated proper test-taking techniques.

What would have been the outcome if I didn't have my mother advocating for my second chance at life? What if I wasn't allowed the opportunity to develop those game-changing test strategies in that new school environment?

How many what-if scenarios have you experienced where the complete trajectory of your life could have been different - for better or worse? Scenarios like the type from my high school years are familiar to many professionals desperately trying to climb the corporate ladder of success.

They go to work full of talent and potential but haven't been given the strategies to succeed in an environment wrought with bias. Regardless of their skill sets, these professionals feel unfairly placed in a box by the corporate system that has seemed to permanently seal their fate - the same way I felt when I didn't pass the CXC exam the first time.

They look around and see the potential of their colleagues being nurtured and accomplishments recognized while they remain overlooked. Over time, these once promising professionals can grow hardened and embittered, accepting their lot as those whose dreams and aspirations go unfulfilled, receiving meager wage increases and lateral moves, while their often less-talented counterparts excel.

Won't things get better if they just work harder? That's the question of many on the outside looking in. Why would someone who knows they have so much to offer settle for less than they know they deserve?

Hard work isn't always enough. Based on my personal journey and the accounts of many corporate professionals I have encountered along the way, there are three critical factors in the corporate environment that often restrict the advancement of these frustrated professionals.

Cultural and Educational Bias

The status quo makes it convenient for managers and other organizational influencers to gravitate towards professionals of familiar language, cultural upbringing, and educational background. It is a natural human tendency for an individual to favor and be more relational to another person with similar or society-endorsed experiences. This could be anything from graduating from the same university, civic or professional organization membership, or even having an interest in similar hobbies.

Just the same, they may avoid certain colleagues with cultural backgrounds that differ significantly because they don't want to "say something stupid" and risk being labeled racist or insensitive. This creates an unintended consequence of an unlevel playing field in the work environment, because even unintentionally, they may seek out or provide opportunities to people to whom they better relate.

Familiarity should never be the sole deciding or overriding factor in determining whether a professional is equipped with the talent to meet and surpass expectations. This inherent and unconscious bias towards backgrounds familiar to the organization's majority leads to major deficiencies in the diversity of thought that can lead to the greatest innovations and problem-solving.

Skewed Meritocracy System

Although performance review and compensation frameworks may be documented by an organization, the corporate meritocracy system is not streamlined as advertised, so it's difficult to understand how individual performance is judged. This setup fundamentally encourages favoritism and recognition aligned to favored professionals.

Biases in the meritocracy system allow for one professional to be awarded at a disparately lower compensation level than another professional who executed at the same or lower level simply because their training and qualifications are deemed inferior. As coveted as it may be, an Ivy League education doesn't automatically equate to a higher level of performance on the job.

This imbalance of performance accolades restricts some employees' access to promotions at an abnormally lower rate with no consideration for their results or organizational impact.

This, of course, can also be extremely detrimental to the victimized employees' morale and confidence in their abilities, not to mention the financial impact over time. An individual thriving in this biased system is often referred to as mastering unwritten rules. What would be different if the rules were clear and fairly applied to all employees?

Relational Currency

It is well known that professional upward mobility is influenced by the relationships they possess within the organization. It's not who you know, but who knows you. How do you get to know decision- makers?

Often, these bonds are created after hours. From the golf course to happy hour, interacting in more relaxed environments can lead to establishing a likability factor that translates to relational currency. Limitations due to personal preferences and cultural values can place some individuals at a major disadvantage when it comes to building relationships, which could further impact career advancement.

These professionals are confronted with divergent paths strikingly like people from my childhood community whose access to education dictated whether they would escape the frustrating walls of poverty.

Life As A Talent Exclusion Victim

I fully comprehend the pain talent marginalization brings in the workplace because I have experienced it firsthand. Talent exclusion stifles your overall growth and restricts the flow of your creativity. Most notably, you can become a victim of the "dangling-carrot" treatment.

You're told, "If you do XYZ, you will get promoted."

So, you do XYZ and still receive no promotion. Then you think, "If I work twice as hard, they have to promote me." But that doesn't work either. Then you see less- qualified people moving ahead and often ponder why you were not chosen.

Feeling like you don't have what it takes to excel professionally can cause irreparable damage to your life emotionally, physically, and financially. Let's evaluate the potential cumulative financial fallout one would endure after being overlooked for a few annual promotions over the course of 10 years, and as a result, being underpaid relative to counterparts by 20 percent.

That professional would be leaving more than $20,000 on the table based on an annual salary base rate of $100,000, in addition to being subjected to any inflationary cost of living increases.

Besides the hard financial toll, there can be a severe emotional cost we cannot ignore. Imagine coming home every day frustrated about your lack of career advancement at work. Believing that the status quo system will never acknowledge your performance as anything beyond mediocre promotes low morale at work and at home, with potential adverse effects to your health, family, and broader community implications.

In essence, one can conclude that the issue is deeper than one professional not receiving a promotion in a single or consecutive year.

These missed opportunities interfere with multiple dimensions of an employee's existence, such as their ability to provide advanced educational or cultural experiences for their children or to appropriately care for aging relatives.

Are You Paddling Against The Current?

If you have ever found yourself in this place, you know that continuously operating in a system you perceive to be working against you can feel like breathlessly paddling a boat in rough waters against the current with no control over the direction of your vessel. It is easy to feel like a victim when you feel powerless to challenge a system of environmental barriers holding you back.

Maybe you've spoken up about the injustices and been labeled a whiner or a threat. Even if there are corporate initiatives focused on rooting out bias in the workplace, the reality is that these changes often take years to be realized, if at all. No one is coming to save you. You must shift your mindset and strategy from victim to victor and save yourself.

Unlike so many people from the neighborhood, I was able to escape those societal boundaries that counted me out based on the prior failure and deliver a powerful comeback. Confronting the issue, rebuilding my self-confidence, deploying a strategy for success, and walking in a level of resilience allowed me to bounce back from the frustration and embarrassment. This same formula can help you rise above victim status, reclaiming your power over your life and destiny.

Are You Paddling Against The Current?

Nelson Mandela reminded us that, *"There is no passion to be found playing small - in settling for life that is less than the one you are capable of living."*

You can break free from the burden of the mental stress and disrespect caused by being overlooked and undervalued. You don't have to settle for the limitations of your current situation.

You can equip yourself to take that long-awaited leap forward and offer innovative thinking and brilliant ideas that shift you into the territory of greatness. With the right transformation toolkit, you can dismantle the barriers that are holding you back. You can position yourself to be seen in a new light, primed for new possibilities, even if decision-makers don't see you with that potential today. That's why I would like to call you an Undercover Victor.

What Is An Undercover Victor?

Undercover Victors, or *UVs*, are free agents who are no longer sitting on the sidelines but have their talent and creative power fully vested for utilization.

They are cognizant of the potency of their talent when it is applied by their organizations. Unlike victimized professionals, UVs are aware of their strengths and their ability to control their own destinies instead of relinquishing control to external environmental factors.

UVs are business environment disruptors who exude resilience and perseverance like no other. They come from many walks of life, having endured talent marginalization in the corporate environment irrespective of industry sector. The underlying trigger for every Undercover Victor's journey is some form of bias related to race, gender, class system, educational pedigree, or personality profile.

These professionals have invaluable talent, even though they were most likely not raised in the upper echelons of society. They were not exposed to all the fancy connections and "Ivy League" qualifications that could open massive doors to success.

Unfortunately, mainstream diversity and inclusion experts have failed to address the true impact of corporate talent marginalization by focusing strictly on the race component.

What Is An Undercover Victor?

The understanding of the talent exclusion experience needs to evolve beyond race to reflect the reality on the ground and improve the chances that excluded professionals transition to a space of thriving.

When you see the abbreviation "UV," you likely think of ultraviolet light. In fact, the Undercover Victor's journey has a striking similarity to UV light.

Ultraviolet is a form of electromagnetic radiation with a wavelength from 10 to 400 nanometers shorter than that of visible light. Humans can't see it. Invisible ultraviolet holds great promise and is instrumental in solving many of the world's social and environmental challenges, such as the production of vitamin D, mood enhancement, and disinfection and sterilization. UV light illuminates the future, even though it is invisible.

The same can be said of the corporate Undercover Victor (UV). UVs are essential to unlocking the pathway to an organization's success even though they may have gone unnoticed for years.

The Victim To Undercover Victor Transformation

Let's be clear: dealing with systematic and institutional bias in the workplace can feel like an insurmountable obstacle. But as we have covered, the monetary, physical, and emotional costs are too high to simply accept them. I wonder where I would be now if I had accepted my failure of the CXC exam as final. How would that have impacted my son's life?

What about the students and professionals I've been able to mentor and support because I've found a way to push through professional challenges? Those who felt stuck in poverty back in Guyana lacked an effective strategy to move beyond the current limitations. It isn't that they didn't work hard, but what they were doing to try to get ahead wasn't working.

When mentoring Undercover Victors, I share a seven-step transformational toolkit to move from victim to victor. While we don't have the space to cover all of that in this chapter, I invite you to visit **SaskiaChristian.com** to receive access to training as it becomes public. But for now, let's focus on the three power knobs necessary to begin the process.

The Victim To Undercover Victor Transformation

THE THREE POWER KNOBS

RESILIENCE · CONFIDENCE · STRATEGY

Resilience

Resilience is defined as the capacity to recover quickly from difficulties. It is the substance that enables you to manage all that self-defeating energy from workplace disappointments and betrayals and convert frustration into hope through self-motivation. A poor mindset is a key enabler to self-destruction. If you want to succeed professionally, your work isn't just the tasks in your job description.

You must also do the work of healing from the detrimental impact of both professional and personal environments that have created self- doubt and despair. It could go all the way back to the soundtracks playing in your head from seeds of doubt planted by a teacher in grade school to a parent urging you to set more realistic expectations for your future. This process takes time and may require enlisting the support of a trained counselor or therapist.

Please know that you are bigger than your challenges. Chances are, you have already demonstrated resilience in other areas of your life. The muscles you've developed in the past around overcoming difficult situations could be a source of competitive advantage.

If you choose to reclaim your power by turning up the dial on your practice of resilience, today's setbacks could be a setup for greater opportunities.

Confidence

Building your confidence is the second power knob in the professional's personal growth process. Confidence is a feeling of self-assurance arising from one's own abilities and qualities. When your self-confidence is low, you are less likely to go after the opportunities you desire or to even share your ideas freely. The result? All your brilliance will go unnoticed and untapped.

At one point in my career, I was struggling to access opportunities to make the significant contributions I knew I was capable of. When a problem surfaced in the production environment I was working in as a process engineer, I tapped into the unique knowledge base I had around water treatment science.

My skill set was needed, and I made my expertise known without hesitation.

Capitalizing on opportunities to work in your zone of genius is always a confidence booster!

Not only that, but this is also an area that I'm passionate about. My contributions to solving the issue opened the door to a lateral opportunity that began a ripple effect of career success.

I had to be audacious and willing to take a risk to leave the domain where I was comfortable yet undervalued. But exercising the confidence to leave my comfort zone led to a space of greater visibility and more numerous opportunities to make meaningful contributions to the success of the organization.

Think back to a time when you felt unstoppable. What were you doing? Was there a certain skill set that you were utilizing?

Were you focused on your personal or professional development by learning new skills? Feeding your mind with content that motivates and inspires you?

Did you have trusted mentors or confidantes to talk to about your struggles who always provided sound advice? Reconnect with that feeling and the actions that take you there.

Strategy

Lastly, strategy application is the third essential power knob and a key differentiator in leveling the playing field for talent inclusion. You can no longer afford to operate without a strategic plan and expect a favorable outcome. What is your goal? What steps do you need to take to get there over time?

Are there additional skill sets or experiences you need to gain to position yourself more competitively? What relationships do you need to build so that the right people know who you are and what you're capable of?

If you feel like you've been pigeonholed with limited opportunities for advancement, reinvent yourself. How can you inject greater passion or purpose into your work? How can you align yourself with the goals and initiatives that are most important to the organization - even if it isn't a part of your core job?

When I took advantage of the opportunity to leverage my water treatment passion and expertise, it took me on a journey that not only advanced me from tactical to strategic career functionality but also equipped me with a new, demonstrated skill set. These opportunities may not appear overnight, but by finding the intersection between who you are, what you're good at, and what's important to the company, you'll be able to see them clearly when they appear.

RESILIENCE + *Confidence* + Strategy = *Breakthrough* SUCCESS

When your company hired you, it wasn't an act of charity. They brought you into the organization because they knew you had something valuable to offer. But somewhere along the way, the actions, or beliefs of individuals in your path, or culture that defaults to support the status quo got in the way of your ability to fully deliver on that potential.

Or maybe you have been consistently delivering, but not getting the recognition you deserve. If you have started to internalize the effects of that environment to the point that it has caused you to question your abilities or worthiness, it's time for a reset.

Focus on healing yourself from the pain, disappointment, and insecurities of your past and present situations. Close the gaps not only in your technical expertise but also in the soft skills that may prevent others from seeing you as leadership material.

The Victim To Undercover Victor Transformation

Step outside of your comfort zone when it comes to taking risks and building professional relationships. Most importantly, be clear about what success looks like for you and develop a strategy to get there.

Decide that you will no longer be a victim when it comes to your professional trajectory. No matter how many times you feel like you've failed the tests that have been placed before you, there is always another opportunity to come back stronger than before.

I reflect on those adults from my childhood community in Guyana who regrettably had their means of escape from a poverty-stricken state stripped from them. You may not be poor, but there's more to life for you than only getting by. Don't let the frustration of your current environment rob you of the richness of a fulfilling professional life where your talents are valued.

Next Steps

Are you or anyone within your network eager to learn how to break free from your "boxed-in" workplace condition? Are you a seasoned, but frustrated professional fed up with playing small and ready to be seen, valued, and utilized? Are you connected to a professional group committed to helping people succeed? If so, I invite you to visit **SaskiaChristian.com** to learn more about the Undercover Victor Transformational Toolkit and to sign up for access to future resources.

Putting It Into Practice

"You don't have to wait on some outside force to increase your motivation. You have the power to motivate yourself."

VALORIE BURTON

Activate Your UV Superpowers

If you're ready to reclaim your power and transition from victim to Undercover Victor (UV), here are a few practical tips to get you started. To track your progress, consider integrating the actions that resonate with you into your personal development plan.

Practicing Resilience

- Intentionally ingest content that supports a positive mindset, such as podcasts and inspirational videos and music.
- Reflect on the challenges you have overcome in the past and how they have helped to shape the qualities that have served you personally and professionally.
- Support yourself with positive, uplifting people.
- Journal daily to process your experiences and how you intend to respond to them.
- Adopt a meditation practice to help you quit your negative self-talk, anxiety, and overthinking.
- Seek out the support of a therapist and/or life coach.

Boost Your Self-Confidence

Keep a file of your accomplishments. When you have moments where you're doubting yourself, reflect on how amazing you are.

Focus on continuously upgrading your knowledge and skills. Set a goal of reading two personal development or leadership books a month. This can be easily met by listening to audiobooks during your commute or workout.

Check with your local library to see if membership includes audiobook rentals.

Listen to your self-talk. Is your inner voice supportive, or are you beating yourself up? Would you say the things you say to yourself to your best friend?

Reprogram your negative internal chatter with positive affirmations. Read them aloud every day.

Strategic Integration

Develop a deep understanding of your organization's strategy. What are the key priorities? What external factors impact the organization's success?

- How does your department's work impact the organization's performance?
- How can you align your knowledge and skills to the organization's priorities?
- How can you tap into your passions and/or purpose to help the organization achieve its goals?
- Be intentional about managing your personal brand. Does your reputation align with the way you want to be seen? If not, it's time to rebrand yourself.

As you develop new skills, don't forget about soft skills like communication and emotional intelligence.

Saskia Christian

Saskia's life mission is to encourage others personally or professionally upon every encounter. Her passion is to see lives transformed.

She is committed to nurturing the development of underserved youth who are aspiring technologists as well as corporate entry-level professionals. For decades, her coaching of a host of leaders from corporate employees to business owners has brought encouragement, healing, and inspiration with extraordinary life-changing results.

Saskia Christian is a Certified Trauma and Resiliency Life coach, Speaker, International Best-Selling Author of a compilation book and Founder of "BoostThru" life coaching service.

She earned a master's degree in chemical engineering from the New Jersey Institute of Technology.

A visionary leader and certified Project Management Professional with over 17 years of experience in the high-tech sector, she has a track record of driving technical breakthroughs, while helping industry leaders integrate innovative technologies and process methodologies across functional domains and industries.

Through her experiences as a Chemical engineer, industrial water treatment expert, and supply chain professional, she experienced and witnessed the negative impact of talent exclusion on professionals and organizations.

As a result, she became motivated to advise individuals on how to do the internal work and exploit their inherent unique strengths for the leveling of the playing field for talent inclusion.

Saskia is a co-author of 4 book compilations, and an e-course portfolio centered around personal and professional resilient leadership cultivation. She is also an active member of Global Society for Female Entrepreneurs (GSFE) and The Chamber of Commerce where she is involved in two committees, Diversity, Equity and Inclusion and Education and Workforce Development.

She was inducted in 2023 as a Marquis Who's Who Honoree for her empowerment work and activities and later recognized as Marquis Who's Who Top Engineer in 2024.

Her business brand was also featured in Sister Leaders Magazine, Celebrity Boss Magazine, and press release by 400 premium news media outlets such as FOX, CBS, The Times, and NBC.

Founder @BoostThru International Best-Selling Author, Motivational Speaker, Trauma Healing & Resilience Life Coach, Executive Contributor to Brainz Magazine.

You can also find her on her business website, www.boostthru.com and social media platforms using Blinq card link
https://blinq.me/AwNFqsqaOm8o9TyYclHM

She is your go to expert for resilience mastery in the combat of professionals distress for the transformation of setbacks into joyful, passion-filled and purpose- driven comebacks.

Connect With Saskia Christian:
Website: https://www.boostthru.com/about-us/
Email: saskiac@boostthru.com

Notes

Notes

Notes

Printed in the USA
CPSIA information can be obtained
at www.ICGtesting.com
CBHW050110260624
10635CB00024B/535